W9-APP-937

GRAPHIC DINOSAURS

TYRANNOSAURUS

THE TYRANT LIZARD

ILLUSTRATED BY JAMES FIELD

PowerKiDS press.

New York

Published in 2008 by The Rosen Publishing Group, Inc.
29 East 21st Street, New York, NY 10010

Designed and produced by
David West Books

Designed and written by Rob Shone
Editor: Gail Bushnell
Consultant: Steve Parker, Senior Scientific Fellow, Zoological Society of London
Photographic credits: Postdlf, 5t; Quadell, 5bl; iStockphotos.com/Christoph Ermel, 30

Library of Congress Cataloging-in-Publication Data

Shone, Rob.
Tyrannosaurus: the tyrant lizard / Rob Shone.
p. cm. — (Graphic dinosaurs)
Includes index.
ISBN-13: 978-1-4042-3897-8 (library binding) ISBN-10: 1-4042-3897-2 (library binding)
ISBN-13: 978-1-4042-9627-5 (pbk.) ISBN-10: 1-4042-9627-1 (pbk.)
ISBN-13: 978-1-4042-9669-5 (6 pack) ISBN-10: 1-4042-9669-7 (6 pack)
1. Tyrannosaurus rex—Juvenile literature. I. Title.
QE862.S3W469 2008
567.912'9—dc22
                                                    2007010442

Manufactured in China

CONTENTS

 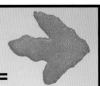

WHAT IS A TYRANNOSAURUS?

TYRANNOSAURUS MEANS "TYRANT LIZARD"

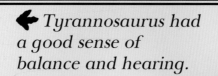

← Tyrannosaurus had a good sense of balance and hearing.

← Tyrannosaurus had a keen sense of smell.

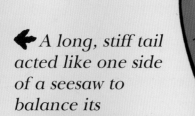

← It had large eyes that faced forward. This helped it judge distances.

← A long, stiff tail acted like one side of a seesaw to balance its massive head.

← Tyrannosaurus's 5-foot (1.5-m) jaws held between 50 and 60 teeth. They grew up to 0.5 feet (0.15 m) long. Their teeth often fell out as they ate but were replaced with new ones throughout their lives.

← Tyrannosaurus's legs had to be strong to carry its huge weight.

← Like all the Tyrannosaurs, Tyrannosaurus had tiny arms.

TYRANNOSAURUS REX LIVED AROUND 70 TO 65 MILLION YEARS AGO, DURING THE **CRETACEOUS** PERIOD. **FOSSILS** OF ITS SKELETON HAVE BEEN FOUND IN NORTH AMERICA.

An adult Tyrannosaurus measured over 40 feet (12 m) long, 16 feet (5 m) high, and weighed 7 tons (6,350 kg).

GROWING UP

Tyrannosaurus rex grew at a steady rate until it was about 13 years old. For the next four or five years it gained 4.4 pounds (2 kg) a day. In that time it went from weighing 1 ton (900 kg) to over 5 tons (4,500 kg). For such a large animal, however, it had a short life. It lived until it was about 30 years of age.

The Tyrannosaurus's teeth were up to 6 inches (15 cm) long. The back edge of each tooth was sharp and wavy, like a steak knife. This made it easier to slice through meat.

A Tyrannosaurus's arms may have been small, but its thick bones supported strong muscles.

FROM HAND TO MOUTH

With its 5-foot (1.5-m) skull and teeth the size and shape of a banana, Tyrannosaurus rex could only have been a meat-eater. It had the strongest bite of any animal and could easily crunch through the biggest bones.

Its two-fingered arms were tiny but powerful. Each one could lift 1 ton (900 kg). They may have been used to grab hold of its **prey** as its teeth went to work.

The American alligator's bite is nearly as powerful as a Tyrannosaurus's bite.

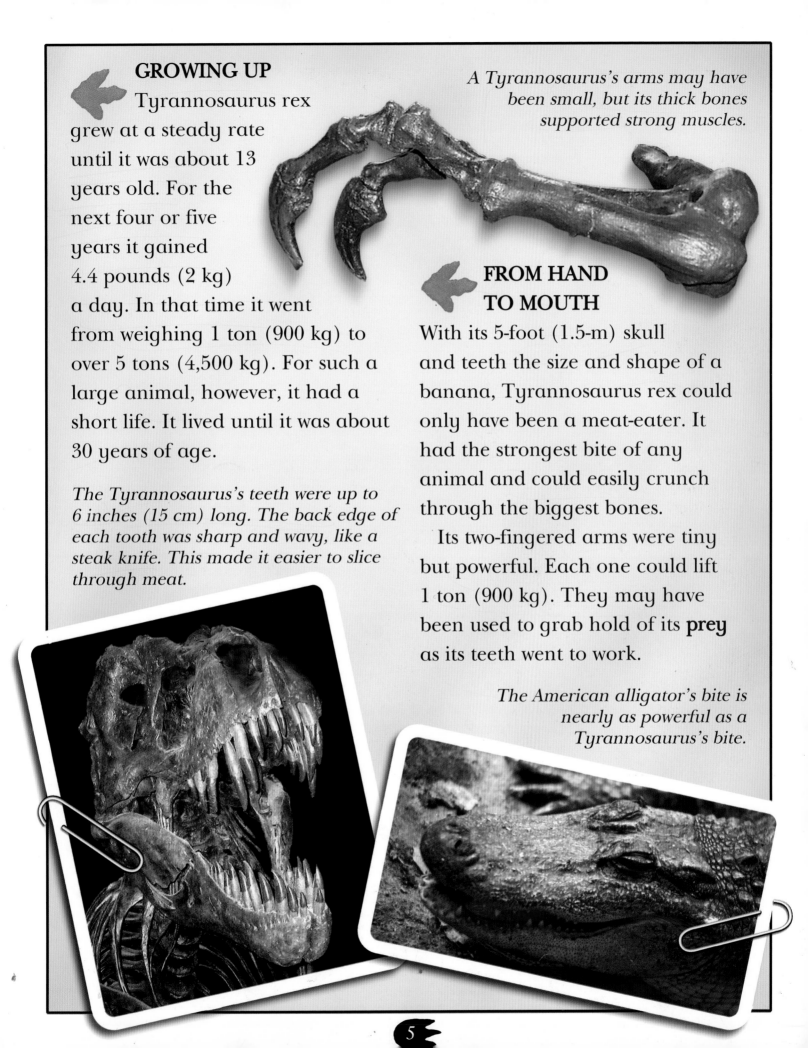

PART ONE

THE LAST EGG

THE BABY TYRANNOSAURUS CREEPS QUIETLY THROUGH THE FOREST.

SUDDENLY, SHE IS AMBUSHED BY ONE OF HER BROTHERS. THEY ARE PLAY-HUNTING.

THEY HEAR A NOISE CLOSE BY AND STOP THEIR PLAY-HUNTING.

THEY HIDE AND WAIT.

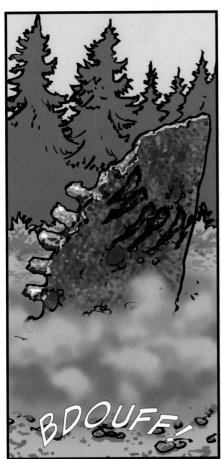

BDOUFF!

THE NOISE HAS BEEN MADE BY THE **HATCHLINGS'** MOTHER. SHE HAS BEEN HUNTING FOR REAL AND HAS RETURNED WITH FOOD FOR THEM.

SHARRGH!

HISSSS!

THE MOTHER TYRANNOSAURUS LEAVES THE HATCHLINGS TO THEIR MEAL.

SHE WANTS TO VISIT HER NEST. MOST OF HER EGGS HAVE HATCHED, BUT THERE MAY BE SOME LEFT.

SHE PUTS HER NOSE INTO THE NEST AND SNIFFS. IT FEELS TOO WARM. THE EGGS WILL NOT HATCH IF THE NEST BECOMES TOO HOT OR TOO COLD.

SHE BLOWS THE WARM EARTH AWAY FROM THE NEST.

PFHOOOF

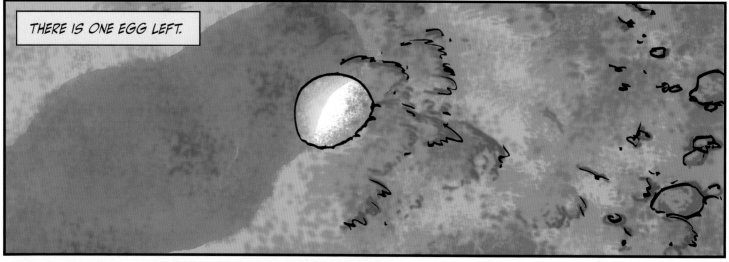

THERE IS ONE EGG LEFT.

SHE WILL RETURN TO THE NEST BEFORE IT GETS DARK AND COVER THE EGG IN THE WARM SOIL.

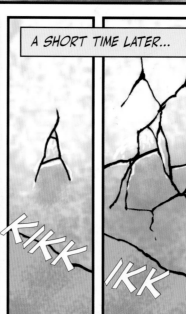

A SHORT TIME LATER...

KIKK IKK KRIKK!

BREAKING OUT OF HIS EGG HAS MADE THE NEW HATCHLING TIRED.

HIS OLDER BROTHERS AND SISTERS GATHER AROUND.

THEY ARE HUNGRY AGAIN.

THEIR MOTHER ARRIVES JUST IN TIME. SHE GENTLY PUSHES THE HATCHLINGS AWAY FROM THEIR NEW BROTHER.

THE LAST HATCHLING WILL SOON BE BIG ENOUGH TO PLAY-HUNT WITH HIS BROTHERS AND SISTERS.

ARRKK!

IT IS ONE YEAR LATER. THERE ARE ONLY FOUR HATCHLINGS LEFT. THEY ARE 3 FEET (1 M) LONG AND CATCH MOST OF THEIR OWN FOOD NOW.

THE LAST HATCHLING HAS CAUGHT A LIZARD. HIS BROTHERS AND SISTERS ARE TRYING TO TAKE IT AWAY FROM HIM.

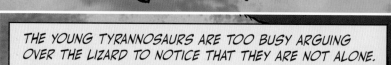

THE YOUNG TYRANNOSAURS ARE TOO BUSY ARGUING OVER THE LIZARD TO NOTICE THAT THEY ARE NOT ALONE.

RHARRK!

THE FULL-GROWN ATROCIRAPTOR IS NO MATCH FOR EVEN ONE OF THE HATCHLINGS. THE YOUNG TYRANNOSAURS TRY TO SCARE IT AWAY.

THEN...

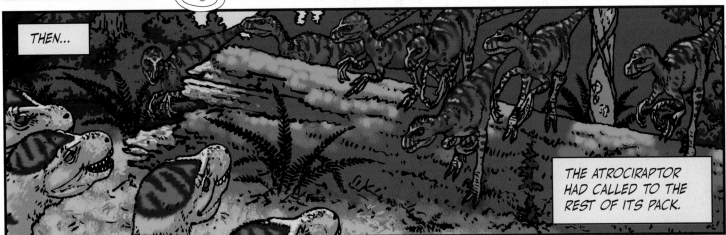

THE ATROCIRAPTOR HAD CALLED TO THE REST OF ITS PACK.

A WHOLE PACK OF ATROCIRAPTORS IS DANGEROUS. THEY WANT THE LIZARD. TOGETHER THEY COULD KILL A TYRANNOSAURUS HATCHLING.

SUDDENLY, FROM THE FOREST...

THUD! THUD! THUD!

THUD!

IT IS A CHIROSTENOTES, AND IT IS BEING FOLLOWED.

THUD!

THUD!

ROOARR!

THE ATROCIRAPTORS ARE SCARED AWAY. EVEN THE YOUNG TYRANNOSAURS RUN AS THEIR ANGRY MOTHER CHASES THE CHIROSTENOTES, WHO HAS TRIED TO STEAL AN EGG.

THUD!

IT IS THE LAST TIME THE HATCHLINGS' MOTHER WILL COME TO THEIR RESCUE. SHE HAS A NEW NEST AND NEW EGGS TO CARE FOR. THE YOUNG TYRANNOSAURS WILL HAVE TO LOOK AFTER THEMSELVES NOW.

IT IS SEVEN YEARS LATER. THE YOUNG TYRANNOSAURS ARE NOW 15 FEET (5 M) LONG. THEY HUNT IN A PACK.

ONCE THEY HAVE SPOTTED THEIR PREY, THEY SPLIT INTO TWO GROUPS.

THEY HAVE SEEN A HERD OF PACHYCEPHALOSAURS. ONE PAIR OF TYRANNOSAURS RUNS AT THE PREY.

THE OTHER PAIR WAITS. WHEN THE PACHYCEPHALOSAURS ARE NEAR ENOUGH THEY WILL RUSH OUT FROM THEIR HIDING PLACE AND AMBUSH THEM.

THE HERD IS DRIVEN FORWARD...

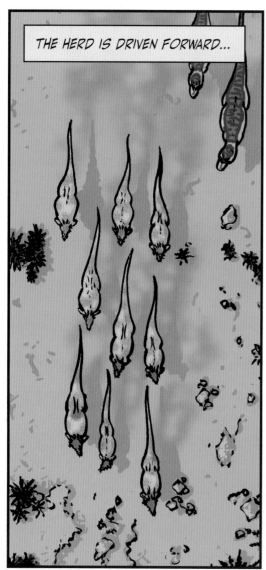

...INTO THE PATH OF THE AMBUSHERS.

THE PACHYCEPHALOSAURS RUN IN *PANIC.*

ONE OF THE PACK CATCHES A STRAY PACHYCEPHALOSAUR, WHEN SUDDENLY...

...THE TYRANNOSAURUS IS HIT BY A CHARGING PACHYCEPHALOSAURUS, AND THEN ANOTHER ONE.

DOUFF!!

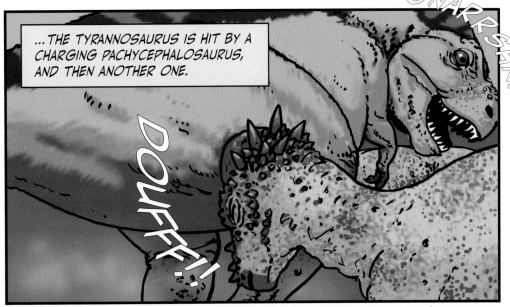

AGAIN AND AGAIN THEY ATTACK, RUNNING AWAY BEFORE THE TYRANNOSAURUS CAN STRIKE BACK.

THE TYRANNOSAURUS IS BADLY HURT. HE CANNOT STAND UP.

THE OTHERS LEAVE AND FOLLOW THE TRAIL OF THE WOUNDED PACHYCEPHALOSAUR. THEY WILL NEVER SEE THEIR BROTHER AGAIN.

THE TYRANNOSAURS ARE NOW 14 YEARS OLD. THEY ARE GROWING VERY QUICKLY AND ARE ALWAYS HUNGRY. THEY NEED TO HUNT LARGER PREY. THE ALAMOSAURUS IS TOO BIG EVEN FOR AN ADULT TYRANNOSAUR, BUT IT IS THE JUVENILE THEY ARE AFTER.

TWO OF THE PACK TRY TO KEEP THE ADULT ALAMOSAURUS BUSY.

BROUAARR!!

THEY NEED TO BE CAREFUL, THOUGH.

BOOUUFF!

THEY HAVE MANAGED TO SEPARATE THE PARENT FROM THE YOUNG ALAMOSAURUS.

THE YOUNG ALAMOSAURUS IS HELPLESS. THE PACK LEADER MOVES IN.

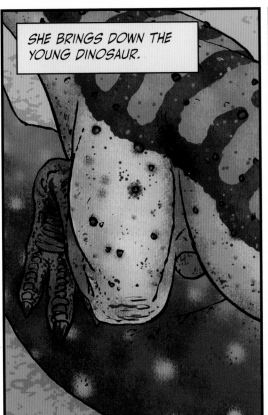

SHE BRINGS DOWN THE YOUNG DINOSAUR.

THE ALAMOSAURUS PARENT REALIZES IT HAS LOST AND LEAVES. THE TWO TYRANNOSAURS GO TO GET THEIR SHARE OF THE MEAT.

THE PACK LEADER WILL NOT LET THE OTHERS NEAR THE KILL. SHE WANTS IT ALL FOR HERSELF.

SHE FIGHTS FOR IT.

THE LARGE FEMALE IS TOO BIG FOR THE OTHERS TO BEAT.

THE PACK SPLITS UP.

PART THREE... HOME TERRITORY

THE LAST HATCHLING IS ENJOYING HIMSELF IN THE WARM MORNING SUN. A FLOCK OF BIRDS ARE CLEANING HIS SCALY SKIN OF TINY INSECTS THAT MAKE IT ITCH.

HE IS NEARLY FULL-GROWN. IT HAS BEEN THREE YEARS SINCE THE PACK SPLIT UP. HE HAS SPENT THE TIME WANDERING FROM PLACE TO PLACE. HE WILL NOT SPEND TOO LONG IN ANOTHER TYRANNOSAURUS'S *TERRITORY*. A LARGER TYRANNOSAURUS MIGHT KILL HIM.

HE HAS BEEN TO THE OCEAN BEFORE.

HE SNAPS AT A NYCTOSAURUS BUT MISSES.

HE SEES SOMETHING EASIER TO CATCH.

A GROUP OF PARKSOSAURUS HAVE LEFT THEIR FOREST HOME.

THE TYRANNOSAURUS MOVES CAREFULLY TOWARD THE SMALL DINOSAURS. HE CANNOT LET THEM SEE HIM.

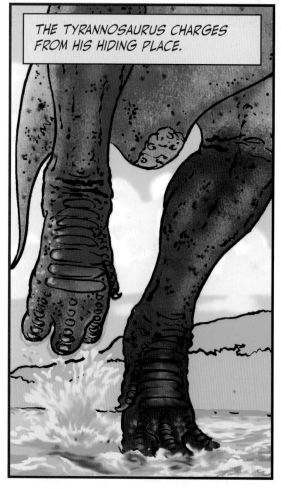

THE TYRANNOSAURUS CHARGES FROM HIS HIDING PLACE.

THE PARKSOSAURUS ARE TOO QUICK. THEY DISAPPEAR BACK INTO THE FOREST.

NOT LONG AGO HE MIGHT HAVE CAUGHT ONE. NOW HE HAS GROWN TOO BIG TO RUN QUICKLY. HE SEES A FLOCK OF ICHTHYORNIS. SOMETHING HAS EXCITED THEM.

THE SEA HAS WASHED UP A DEAD TURTLE.

THE TYRANNOSAURUS DRAGS THE GIANT TURTLE FROM THE WATER.

GERCRUNCH!

THE SHELL OF THE TURTLE IS HARD. THE TYRANNOSAURUS'S SIZE HAS MADE HIM SLOW, BUT IT HAS GIVEN HIM A STRONG BITE.

HE MOVES INLAND UP A RIVER MOUTH. HE CAN SMELL FRESH BLOOD.

THE SMELL LEADS HIM TO A WOOD. A YOUNG FEMALE TYRANNOSAURUS HAS A DEAD HADROSAUR.

THE FEMALE LETS OUT A WARNING ROAR WHEN SHE SEES THE NEWCOMER.

GROAARR!

THE TWO MEAT-EATERS ARE AS BIG AS EACH OTHER.

GNARRHH!

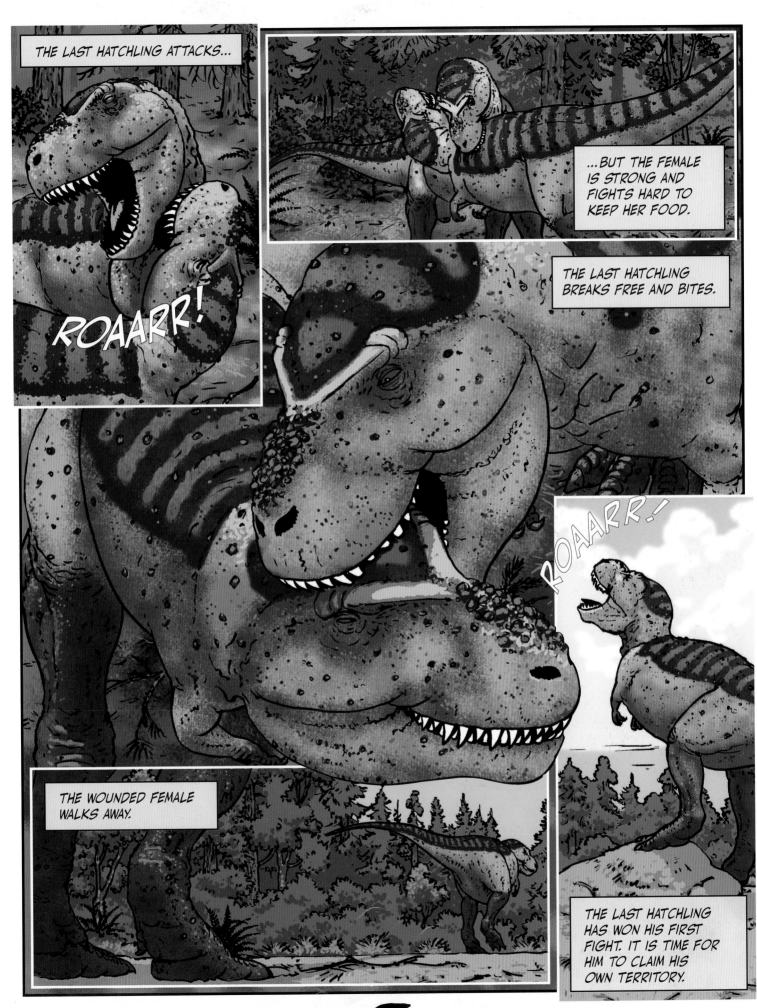

THE LAST HATCHLING ATTACKS...

...BUT THE FEMALE IS STRONG AND FIGHTS HARD TO KEEP HER FOOD.

THE LAST HATCHLING BREAKS FREE AND BITES.

ROAARR!

ROAARR!

THE WOUNDED FEMALE WALKS AWAY.

THE LAST HATCHLING HAS WON HIS FIRST FIGHT. IT IS TIME FOR HIM TO CLAIM HIS OWN TERRITORY.

PART FOUR

THE FIRE

THREE EDMONTOSAURS SLOWLY WANDER THROUGH THE FOREST. THEY DO NOT KNOW THAT THEY ARE IN GREAT DANGER.

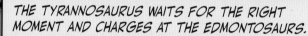

THE LAST HATCHLING IS NOW A 20-YEAR-OLD ADULT. HE HAS BEEN WATCHING THE THREE DINOSAURS. HE MIGHT NOT BE ABLE TO RUN QUICKLY, BUT HE KNOWS HOW TO AMBUSH THEM.

THE TYRANNOSAURUS WAITS FOR THE RIGHT MOMENT AND CHARGES AT THE EDMONTOSAURS.

GRAHH!

WARHHK!

THE EDMONTOSAURUS MANAGES TO WRIGGLE FREE AND RUNS.

THE TYRANNOSAURUS CHASES AFTER IT.

THE EDMONTOSAURUS DASHES INTO A RIVER.

THE TYRANNOSAURUS DOES NOT FOLLOW. THE AIR SMELLS STRANGE.

THE TYRANNOSAURUS CAN SMELL SMOKE. NOT FAR AWAY A SMALL FIRE HAS GROWN INTO A LARGE ONE. THE FIRE IS MOVING QUICKLY TOWARD HIM.

ANIMALS THAT USUALLY RUN AWAY FROM HIM RUSH PAST, TRYING TO ESCAPE FROM THE FLAMES.

THE TYRANNOSAURUS REALIZES HE IS IN DANGER.

THE TYRANNOSAURUS RUNS
THROUGH THE FLAMES...

...AND INTO THE RIVER.

THE FIRE GETS CLOSER AND CLOSER.

THERE IS NOWHERE ELSE
TO GO.

LATER, THE TYRANNOSAURUS COMES OUT FROM BEHIND THE WATERFALL. IT HAS SAVED HIS LIFE.

HE CAN LEAVE NOW THAT THE FIRE IS OUT.

ALL THE TREES ARE BURNED. HIS TERRITORY IS COVERED WITH GRAY ASH. IT WILL BE MANY WEEKS BEFORE NEW PLANTS GROW AND ANIMALS RETURN.

HE CAN SMELL MEAT.

A HADROSAUR HAS BEEN KILLED BY THE FIRE. IT WILL FEED THE TYRANNOSAURUS FOR SEVERAL DAYS. THEN HE WILL HAVE TO MOVE ON AND FIND A NEW TERRITORY TO RULE OVER.

FOSSIL EVIDENCE

SCIENTISTS LEARN WHAT DINOSAURS MAY HAVE LOOKED LIKE BY STUDYING THEIR FOSSIL REMAINS. FOSSILS ARE FORMED WHEN THE HARD PARTS OF AN ANIMAL OR PLANT BECOME BURIED AND TURN TO ROCK OVER MILLIONS OF YEARS.

Scientists are not sure whether Tyrannosaurus rex was a hunter or a **scavenger** or both. When an Edmontosaurus skeleton in the Denver Museum in Colorado was looked at, scientists noticed that part of its tail had been bitten. They saw that the shape of the bite was the same as a Tyrannosaurus's mouth. They also saw that the bones had begun to heal. The Edmontosaurus must have been alive when the Tyrannosaurus attacked it. It must also have escaped the attack. Tyrannosaurus rex may have scavenged, but it could also hunt.

We do know that Tyrannosaurus fought its own kind. Their fossil skeletons show injuries that could only have been caused by another Tyrannosaurus. One skeleton, nicknamed Stan, has a 1-inch (2.5-cm) hole in the back of his skull. A Tyrannosaurus tooth fits neatly into it. The bite did not kill him, though.

DINOSAUR GALLERY

ALL THESE ANIMALS APPEAR IN THE STORY.

Atrociraptor
"Cruel thief"
Length: 3 ft (1 m)
A small, feathered dinosaur with a **retractable** claw on each of its first toes.

Chirostenotes
"Narrow hand"
Length: 7 ft (2 m)
A fast-moving meat-eater with very long hands.

Nyctosaurus
"Bat lizard"
Wingspan: 10 ft (3 m)
Not a dinosaur but a flying reptile.

Parksosaurus
"Parks's lizard"
Length: 8 ft (2.4 m)
A small plant-eater with a beak instead of front teeth.

Pachycephalosaurus
"Thick-headed lizard"
Length: 18 ft (5.5 m)
A plant-eater with a very thick and bony skull.

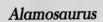

Alamosaurus
"Alamo lizard"
Length: 68 ft (21 m)
A giant plant-eating dinosaur weighing 30 tons (27,216 kg).

Edmontosaurus
"Edmonton lizard"
Length: 43 ft (13 m)
A large plant-eater named after the place in Canada where its fossils were first found.

GLOSSARY

ambushed (AM-bushd) Attacked by surprise from a hiding place.

Cretaceous period (krih-TAY-shus PIR-ee-ud) The time between 146 million and 65 million years ago.

fossils (FAH-sulz) The remains of living things that have turned to rock.

hatchlings (HACH-lingz) Young animals that have hatched from eggs.

juvenile (JOO-vuh-nyl) A young animal that is not full-grown.

panic (PA-nik) To be suddenly scared.

prey (PRAY) Animal that is hunted and killed for food by another animal.

retractable (ree-TRAK-ta-bull) Something that can be drawn back.

scavenger (SKA-ven-jur) An animal that feeds on other animals that are already dead.

territory (TER-uh-tor-ee) An area of land that an animal controls.

INDEX

Web Sites
Due to the changing nature of Internet links, The Rosen Publishing Group, Inc., has developed an online list of Web sites related to the subject of this book. This site is updated regularly. Please use this link to access the list:
www.powerkidslinks.com/gdino/tyran/